The Valley Is Not Your Home

a collection of poems
by Janelle Maree

Copyright © 2018 Janelle Maree
All rights reserved
ISBN: 978-0-9991079-1-1

Yaweh, Jehovah, Redeemer, my Grace, may this book be a testimony, a hallelujah, a match with a greedy flame, an old and rusty lantern that somehow never goes out. May it be a thank You for calling me back home every time I ran away, every time that I tried to hide from You. Thank You for never keeping Your Grace from me.

May these poems be a thank You for putting these words on my heart and telling me exactly what to do with them, giving me a gift I spent years refusing to accept; a gift that I spent years too afraid to use. I've stopped running long enough to finally open it, use the wrapping to bandage my wounds and ultimately, create this book.

*May it be a hymn that will forever sing thank You again and again.
Amen, amen, amen.*

Contents

Forward	1
Welcome Home	2
Essay	6
The Last Word	7
Jeremiah 29:11	8
Baggage Claim	10
The Bird Who Forgot How To Sing	12
An Ode To Hope	14
Essay	16
This Poem Is An Apology	18
Essay	20
A Thank You To The Sea	22
Grieving By Numbers	24
Gone But Not Forgotten	26
Barbara	28
Celeste	29
Practice Makes Forgiveness	30
Let It Go	31
Sticks & Stones	32
Heart Of A Warrior	33
People Are Not Burdens	34
Unconditional	36
Road Trips And Hot Chocolate	38
Mosaics Too Are Beautiful	40

Hope Will Know My Name	42
Difficult To Believe; Extraordinary	44
You Are Not Alone In This	45
Sincerely Yours	46
A Sigh Of Relief	48
Take Hold	50
Ok, Cupid	54
If My Words Spoke As Loud As My Actions	56
I Don't Want To Be A Thorn In Your Side Anymore	58
The Great Quake Of 2018	62
The Valley	66
Shock Trauma	68
Bittersweet Thank Yous	72
Essay	78
This Poem Is Another Apology	80
Interwoven Hope	84
It's A Shame	85
Post-it Notes As A Form Of Coping	86
Essay	92
IP57	96
I am, I am, I am	98
Where The Heart Is	100
Acknowledgements	103

Forward

There is not a cure for sadness buried in these poems, no answer for depression and despair, but I hope that you can still find comfort here. These poems are not about getting happy. They are about coming home. They are about choosing joy. That takes a lot of practice. Sometimes we have to start with just going through the motions, but I've found that if I immerse myself in joyful things for long enough they eventually seep into my skin. It takes time and work and that's the point in these poems. They say, "Take the time. Put in the work." These poems ask, "How will you practice joy? When we find ourselves lost in dark and lonely places what is it that turns on the light? What leads us out?" When pain has me unable to see the next step in front of me, when the darkness is overwhelming these poems remind me, I will not settle in. I will not dwell in it until my eyes adjust. The valley is not where I belong. The valley is not my home.

Hopelessness is not a part of us. Loneliness and sorrow are not our destinies. It is in our nature to find where we belong, to come home; to search for it like a moth in the night, like a way out of a cave we've lost ourselves in. These poems remind me to search for the light, to keep searching for it, to find joy, to not give up, to not lose hope. They remind me that I always find my way home. They remind me I have learned my way in the dark to lead others out.

Welcome Home

Janelle, the valley is not your home.
You will not grow old here.
You come here to mourn;
you'll leave when you are ready.
This place is not a part of you.
You can begin the healing process here.
This place will teach you how to grieve,
it will teach you what to say
when someone else is hurting,
but it is not long term.
It is not your destination.
It is not the finish line for you.
You deserve a better view.
Your story does not end here;
there are so many more pages waiting to be written,
there will be more chapters,
this is only one chapter,
you have an entire series ahead of you.
This is not a place to make yourself comfortable.
I know, it feels familiar.
You reach its lowest point,
you recognize the scenery,
but that does not mean you must live there.
That does not make a home.
You do not have a foundation here.
You will not build yourself walls here;
that would only keep your loved ones from reaching you.
They are here for you,
they have come to visit,
they want you to come home.
Do not settle down here.
Let them lead you out.
They leave a trail of hope for you to follow.
It looks like memories,
you remember standing front row
as your favorite band
plays your favorite song off your favorite album,
the first time you went to the movies by yourself,
Mad Max: Fury Road
in the crappy Lexington Park theater,

the extra gooey chocolate brownies Shari makes,
the day you met Bethany,
Ciera lying next to you in the street in the pouring rain,
balloons on your birthday,
the cheesecake from New York your family sends you every year,
God listening to you when you are angry,
especially when you are angry,
His patience with you,
His unconditional love for you,
the way He still calls you his daughter
no matter how many times you've run away,
palm trees
and good books,
and sunflowers,
and apple juice,
and road trips to Ohio, Norfolk,
Pittsburgh, New York,
Delaware, Chicago,
and Michigan,
teaching 5-year-old Adisu how to say *spoon,*
and *cupcake* and *crayon* in English,
reading your poetry to strangers
in Tina's living room,
the Pacific Ocean,
The Iron Giant,
forts in the Walker's backyard,
the "I love me" tattoo on the back of your neck,
the way your mother pronounces breakfast,
your students' never-ending love for play-dough,
how you and Kate looked jumping into the bay in February
in matching dolphin t-shirts,
Goonies never say die!
the glow-in-the-dark stars on your ceiling
you bought for yourself when you were 19,
your scars finally healing,
bon fires and inside jokes,
hours of Kidz Bop with Jenna,
and how thankful you are
she's moved on to Bruno Mars,
holiday themed socks,
roller coasters,
sunsets,

the chubby hula girl sitting on the dashboard of your car,
polaroid pictures new and old,
Relient K's Christmas album,
listening to Dan sing along to the radio at the top of his lungs,
a 7-mile hike around the lake,
thinking about what it really means to be at peace,
you remember that all these things
make panic attacks,
and ex-best friends,
screwing up all those second chances,
bad days,
bad haircuts,
bad winters,
punishing yourself,
dropping out of college,
being afraid of so many things and that starting so early,
the 6th time you failed your driver's test,
watching the children you love suffer,
all the judgement,
the suicide attempt,
the broken promises,
the stage fright,
the lies,
the nightmares,
your dad being sent to jail,
the fact that he deserved that,
being diagnosed as Bi-polar,
all the things you regret,
that you wish you could change,
that frustrate you,
embarrass you,
that scare you
bearable.
All these things are bearable
now that you remember
the rest of your story.
These things belong here;
you do not.
You need to remember that.
There is so much more out there.
You cannot stay here.
There is so much more good in your life than bad.

I know the disappointing things,
the terrifying things,
the painful things
take center stage so often.
Sometimes they send you here,
but the hopeful things,
the things that make you laugh,
the memories you cherish,
the God that never gives up on you,
the things that make this place all worth it,
they are calling you home.

I'm honest about the times I've been suicidal because depression is a liar. It tells me I will always feel that way. It tells me and so many of my loved ones that we are alone in feeling this way. Life proves to me again and again that that is not true.

I write a lot of poems about mental illness but they're about hope more than anything. I write poetry because depression is a liar and I want to speak the truth.

I am surrounded by love and support but this illness makes me forget that I am cherished. That there are people whose hearts would ache in my absence. That they would mourn for all that I had brought to their lives. I forget about the pain it would cause my loved ones to only use past tense when speaking of me. I forget that I deserve to take up space in this world. That I have value that cannot be replaced. That if I left early, the place I hold now would stay empty. It would forever echo my name. It would be branded with, "Janelle should be here. There are people who still need her. She had so much left to say."

Depression lies to my friends and to my family and the cashier at CVS and the famous Broadway actor and the retired astronaut and inmates and maybe to the woman who let me know 20 bucks fell out of my pocket in the Walmart parking lot yesterday and kids, yeah even kids. I tell the truth for them. I write to remind myself that at some point I knew the truth well enough to write these poems for later, for when the truth is not so clear. I write in hopes it would reach someone being lied to.

Honesty can be terrifying. Stigma and shame are so deeply ingrained in us. I am not always hopeful. I don't always know how to talk about this stuff. It's scary, and messy. I get emotional. I am an ugly crier. But I speak up anyway. I wrote a book of poems just like this one, anyway.

I'm sharing this poem because I've learned that there is something really powerful about brazenly acknowledging our pain enough to tell each other there was a time when we had reached the end of the line, only to have turned around, and run the other way. Stay. Share your story. Listen to someone else's. We have so much left to say.

The Last Word

I write, I write, I write.
I revised the note so many times
because it had to be just right.
It's rare that I'm left at such a loss for words,
but I can't think of the right way to say this.
I can't bear to have my last words be, "I'm sorry."
I can't bear to have my story summarized
with an apology,
a tragic ending in my own handwriting.
I have so much left to say.
There's no good in this goodbye.
So, I finish my lesson plan,
I text my mom back,
I sign the perfect birthday card for my best friend.
I write this poem instead.

Jeremiah 29:11

The waves crash down over me.
I am fighting off drowning,
but I am growing tired.
I call out to You for help,
asking You to rescue me;
bring me to dry land where I can breathe easily.
I just want to go home.
Instead, I sink into the sea.
The waves overcome me.
I do not understand.
You said You'd never leave me or forsake me.
So why am I drowning?
Why have You let me fall beneath safety?
I begin to panic.
But just as quickly as I doubted You,
You give me the ability to breathe.
I take in water but it tastes like air.
My lungs have adapted to the sea.
This is not the help that I had planned for,
that I expected, that I prayed for.
It's an entirely different story.
I don't understand why I am breathing underwater
when all I asked for was to reach land safely.
You assure me this change in plans
is not a failed rescue attempt or a punishment.
This was Your plan all along.
I will learn here. I will grow.
I may suffer trying to swim home
but more than I will ache, I will heal.
I brought myself so deep into a raging sea
I doubted You could reach me
and even when You did
I acted like the help You gave me just wasn't good enough.
You stay patient with me.
You show me I could never be too far from Your grace.
Peace can find me wherever I am at,
I now know that.
I do not need to be at my best.
I do not need to be on dry land first.
I do not need to have it all together.

I do not need to be prepared.
You have work for me to do here.
There are people who need my help.
There are reasons why You did not rescue me
in the way that I had always pictured.
There are reasons for me to be swimming home
when I begged to walk instead.
There are reasons for me to still be here
that I may never really understand.
It's still an answer to my prayers.
It's not as comfortable as a life vest
and a rescue team.
It's not as grand and beautiful
as You lifting me up
and teaching me to step onto the water
so I could walk home gracefully.
It's not what I planned for
but Your plans are not always aligned with mine.
They don't always make sense to me.
They are rarely the easiest journey.
I don't understand that
and I may never will
but I'm learning that's okay.
Your grace will bring me home anyway.
I asked for an answer to my prayers and You delivered.
I have to stop trying to answer for You.
I've learned maybe it's gonna look different
and maybe it's gonna look scary
and maybe it's gonna look like Nineveh,
or forgiving the person you've hated for a very long time,
or trying something new and frightening,
or leaving behind something you love very, very much.
Maybe it's gonna look like giving up the plans
you had for yourself, for your life.
Maybe it's gonna look like trying your best again and again and again.
Maybe it's gonna look like standing in front of the Red Sea
and asking for something practical like a ship
and in return being asked to watch You part it.
Your plans are greater than my own,
to give me hope and a future.
All I need to plan for is to trust
You enough to follow You home.

Baggage Claim

I carry travel sized issues wherever I go.
Fear of abandonment
pairs nicely with a hesitation to trust.
They are kept beneath both a layer of
codependency and intimacy anxiety,
a constant contradiction,
wrinkled and disheveled,
I wear them every day.
I am beginning to unpack
my baggage on these pages.
Poetry lessens the load.
Handle with care
was scrawled across my skin
in thick black letters
on the day that I was born,
but I was still drawn to the people
who were careless with me.
I chose them over the ones
who tried to wrap their arms around me
so that I would not break.
I don't want to be damaged goods.
I want to send all this luggage away,
but I fear the cost of shipping is too great.
It all feels like too much.
I ask myself what if the weight is too much.
I ask this too much.
I know I can't carry it all on my own.
So, I'm gonna start letting some of it go.
I am using poems.
I write it out as much as I can.
I write as much as I can.
When the burden is light enough
I will keep moving.
I will not pick up any of my baggage
once I set it down.
I will not look for it in lost and found
because I have found
that I have more than I have lost.
Building trust is painful for me
but I brace myself.

I lean in to it.
I try again and again.
It's getting easier.
I am adapting to the pain.
It is worth it.
I fear people will never love me enough
to stay.
So, I either keep my distance,
afraid to not be enough,
afraid to be too much,
or I try begging to be needed,
demanding too much from myself,
desperate to earn love,
pleading for it to be permanent.
I'm learning to stay somewhere in between;
an open door
but a security guard always on duty.
I will not beg anyone to come in and stay anymore.
I can't leave my issues behind
but I am strong enough to carry them
and with every collection of poems
my shoulders find relief.

The Bird Who Forgot How To Sing

I sit in my cage
a canary in a coal mine of anxiety
just waiting for something bad to happen.
I was captured as a child,
a beautiful little thing,
with so many songs to sing
until my freedom was taken from me.
When I first realized I had no room to
spread my wings
I broke them trying to get free.
They never healed quite right,
so eventually I just stopped fighting.
I thought I was better off trapped
than living a life with pain in every flight.
What kind of bird would I be
with such flawed things attached to me?
I stayed behind those bars long enough to forget
that I was supposed to want to leave.
I forgot how to sing.
I accepted my fate,
but then one day anxiety forgot to lock my cage.
I was afraid but not enough to stay.
I was ready to be brave.
So, I spread my bent and broken wings,
finally free.
I began to sing a song of victory
as I flew, crooked, pained, and hopeful
toward the light at the end of the tunnel.

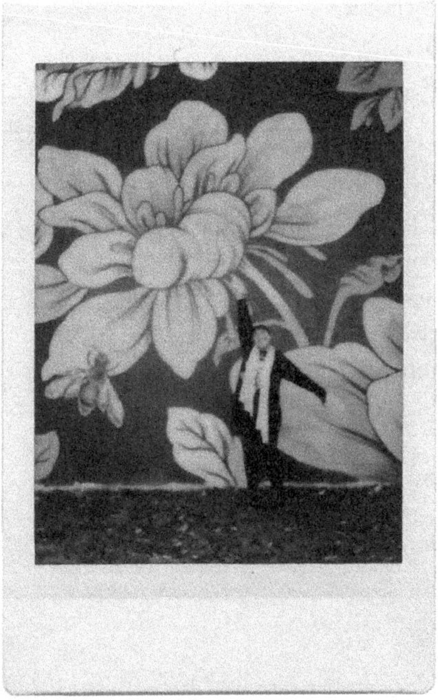

An Ode To Hope

Hope saved me.
I want to share it.
I want to advertise for it.
I want to promise it to you.
I want to see it spread like a wildfire,
like a child's grin from ear to ear,
like migration across the sky,
like colors in the autumn leaves,
like the tide when it is rising,
watercolor on a canvas,
warmth in an embrace,
rain in April,
the light at dawn,
your fingers through your lover's hair,
goosebumps on your flesh when you are scared,
your favorite song through the speakers,
prayers in times of tragedy.
I want it to spread just like it did
when it grew through every bone in my body.
I want it to eat away at sadness,
charge at fear,
rescue you from sorrow and despair.
Let it catch you.
Swallow it whole.
Let it heal you.
Just don't keep it to yourself;
let it grow.

to whom it may concern

I learned about depression and social/general anxiety when I was just kid. I went through various stages of severity with both. I've been suicidal. I've been housebound. I can't remember ever not struggling with mental illness. I had to educate myself. I had to educate others. I had to learn to love myself through it. I had to gather the strength to face it every day. It took me almost 16 years to accept my brain exactly the way it is. It took me so long to accept that I would not be cured, that my illnesses were chronic, that this was just something I had to live with. I learned it was something I could fight every day that I could still win without being cured. I decided that my life could still have purpose, I could still reach goals, I was still valuable. Life would still be worth living in spite of all the pain. I spent years fighting against shame and stigma until I could speak my truth out loud. My illness is not a secret. I tell the truth, I speak out to help others, I teach and I continue to learn. This was the hardest thing I've ever done but so, so worth it.

Recently the diagnosis that I had feared, since I was a pre-teen, that I had lied to get away from for so long, that I felt was just too much, had finally caught up to me. Bi-polar disorder, bi-polar 2 to be specific. Depression paired with hypomania. My worst fear, a reality. It had always been a reality but denial had become my close friend. I felt like I was back at square one. I hated myself again. I was swallowed whole by shame. The new stigma I was being asked to fight was just too strong. After all that work, I was furious, devastated. I felt I had betrayed myself by finally being honest with my doctors. I had led them right to the truth and now I had to face it. You'd think I could bring the new diagnosis into the group and keep going but it brought a new, heavier batch of stigma. It felt too heavy. I didn't think I could do another 16 years of trying to conquer this shame.

I was overwhelmed. People wouldn't understand. I barely understood myself. People would judge me. I judged myself. The word bi-polar was used insensitively and incorrectly all the time. It's another word for crazy, people use it as an insult, people demonize it and also trivialize it. It was such a hard battle I was being asked to fight. There was no way of escaping that. How could I possibly wade through all the stigma and reach any kind of acceptance from myself and others.

My choice was to lie, or fight. I've done enough lying and it never did me any good. I'm doing my best to get in the ring every day. To keep my chin down and throw a good punch. It's hard, I'm tired and it's only been a year and a half of this, I may have another 15 to go. Maybe not, I've had a lot of practice. I've learned a lot the hard way. I know enough to help others; maybe I can take my own advice this time. I'm trying, one day at a time. I think it's worth it. I think my honesty about my anxiety, my depression; I think it's helped other people. I know it helped me. Maybe this story can help too. Declaring my flaws as nothing to be ashamed of, turning my honesty into poetry, it was powerful and cathartic. It took a very, very long time, but maybe this time it won't hurt for quite as long. I think it's gonna be painful. I think I'm gonna be embarrassed often, but there's a sense of relief too. I told a lot of lies; I'm done with that. I wasn't getting the right kind of help; I am now. My actions, my emotions didn't make any sense; they do now. I'm just getting started but these things help. My faith helps, my mom helps, my friends help, the coping skills I worked so hard to master, they still help.

I'm doing my best to be gentle with myself, to show myself more grace than I have in the past, to be brave, to speak up, to do it often and to do it loud. I never know who may be listening, who may need to hear my story. I'm doing my best to be unashamed, to be completely myself. I have bi-polar disorder. I'm not a monster. I am not crazy. I am not a stereotype. I am more than just my illness; I am a daughter, a sister, a friend, a teacher, a poet. I have joy and faith and I know hope well. I am compassionate. I am kind. I love and I am loved. My life is valuable. I am worthy. I am going to be okay, I'm going to be just fine.

This Poem Is An Apology

Forgive me, Janelle
for all the moments you wanted to speak up
but I demanded you stay silent.
I told you to not be that girl,
and it's just a joke,
and why are you always so offended,
you're too damn sensitive,
and maybe they didn't even mean it,
and maybe they did
but shut up, shut up, shut up.
I drove you past the scene of a crime
and as you reached for your phone
I assured you someone else
would make the call.
Forgive me, Janelle
for every single time
I sliced through your skin
like tape on a package
looking for relief inside.
I only found another thing
for you to cry about.
I donated your blood
but you're the one who needed help.
I see that now.
I thought I was taking care of you
when I traced over your scars
as if refusing to mark any new territory
would stop you from noticing
how your scars never really did get old.
Forgive me, Janelle
for telling you to be with him
if only to make it so your father
wasn't the only man
to have every touched you.
As if that boy's hands could have rinsed you clean.
I didn't know the nightmares would come back.
I didn't know you would come out of this
with regret and not redemption.
I didn't know you would never again ask to be held.

I didn't know enough about PTSD or really,
I didn't care enough to notice all the warning signs;
your body clothed in caution tape,
your mind scrambling to lock the door.
Forgive me, Janelle
For telling you bi-polar just meant crazy.
For all the years I told you
that you were both too much
and never enough.
For pushing away the people
who just wanted to take care of you.
For telling you to lie to your doctors
and your mother and your friends.
For teaching you to hold a grudge against God.
For convincing you your fears were stronger
than you'd ever be.
For lying when I said taking medication
was a sign of weakness.
For making you ashamed of yourself.
For making you believe
depression was an inescapable death sentence.
For all the times I said the pain was not worth it.
For telling you hope was foolish.
For acting like you didn't deserve better.
For not apologizing sooner.

I used to want self-care to be prettier and more consistent. I wanted it to be a better show. Less, "I took my medication today," and more, "I went on a road trip with friends!" I thought it would start with drinking a large glass of water and go up from there to a bubble bath, making lunch plans with a friend, getting a manicure and just plain old feeling better because I did a couple nice things for myself. And sometimes it does look like that. Sometimes it's getting a new haircut and redecorating my room and having a sleepover with my friends; very cute stuff, very look at me being so kind to myself, inspirational Facebook post kind of stuff. Those are really great things to do when you are sad and hurting but sometimes I'm just not ready for that yet.

It's okay if taking care of yourself looks boring sometimes like cancelling plans or taking a vitamin, or feels embarrassing like putting clean clothes on for the first time in a few days or private, something you choose to do completely alone without help or Instagram. It's okay if it feels selfish. Yeah, sometimes it is okay to be selfish. If the thought of girl's night out makes you feel like you're being asked to hike Mt. Everest with a sprained ankle, it's okay to cancel. It's okay to reschedule. It's okay to skip it. Sure, they'll be disappointed, they'll miss you but that's okay. You can put yourself first this time.

Yesterday taking care of myself meant letting my body sleep until 3 p.m. and then dragging it to the grocery store with my mom for an hour and then, you know what? I went right back to bed. It looked like baby steps and small victories and knowing when to push yourself and when not to, and that getting back into bed is not the same thing as giving up.

Today it looks like waking up early and hiking a couple miles. That sounds like self-care 101, right? But it's also probably gonna look like sleeping for 13 hours afterwards because you can't shock your body out of depression by going from 0 to 60. That isn't the plan anyway. Today's agenda is to switch up the reasons my body is aching. Tonight, my muscles will be sore not from lying in the same position for days but because I climbed a lot of hills. That looks like compromise and trying something new even if it hurts and it looks like team work between my brain and my body. Yeah, even if it ends up with me back in bed.

Tomorrow I hope self-care looks like something fun but maybe it'll just be deep conditioning the knots out of my hair and, hey, maybe it's just more sleeping until I'm ready to get up and try again.

Just remember depression itself is demanding enough. It asks so much of us and our bodies. If you demand a smooth, pretty, linear recovery from yourself you're going to be disappointed and frustrated and you're gonna feel like you're failing.

Self-care can look like makeovers and pizza parties and treating yourself, but it also looks like picking up your new prescription, avoiding triggers, going to talk to your counselor for the second time in a week, crying out to God, doing some laundry, and making plans to face the world again tomorrow even if that just means you set your alarm for 3 p.m. We are all just trying to do our best here and depression doesn't want you to remember that your best is good enough. But that's all self-care really is, trying your best and letting that be enough.

A Thank You To The Sea

I sit near the ocean
connecting the dots along my skin
that are the summer's freckles and the beach's sand.
The sun leaves lines of color across my body.
I am shades of amber. I am painted by the light.
I feel at home here.
The waves are loud enough to quiet the intrusive thoughts
I am better off without,
but the good memories refuse to be silenced.
I welcome them with open arms as I wade into the sea.

As we pretend the river is an ocean
you take my hand and we stand tall upon the rocks.
You remind me of how far I've come,
how much I tried, how hard I fought.
I speak of being thankful to be alive,
of being grateful we survived.
I believe that we can cope, that this is all worth it.
I say, "I think it's all worth it."
Your voice cracks. It is a brave sound.
You tell me, "I feel that way too."
The waves crash as we bask in second chances.

The sun rinses its paintbrush in the ocean
as the waves reach up to meet me.
I am flooded by these memories.
A smile grows across my face
like the sunset's strokes of colors spread across the sky.
I remember how I've changed, how I've grown.
I remember my loved ones
and how they've joined me in embracing honesty and hope.
I remember shame is a heavy burden to carry.
I remember that it's okay to let it go
and with that thought echoing in my ears
I say, "I am so happy to be home"
as I take a breath and dive into the sea.

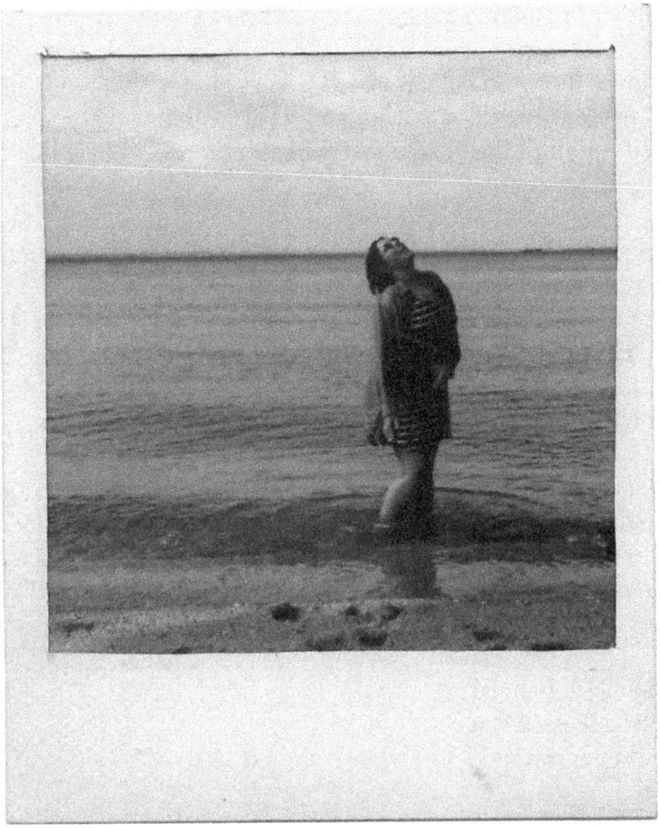

Grieving By Numbers

1. Denial looks like my lips being tightly sewn shut. I cannot speak my truth. My heart doesn't mean to be cruel it's just trying to protect itself. It takes the thread and pulls it tightly until it hurts so much I forget what I was trying to say. My heart says I'm ready now. It snips the thread keeping my voice locked away, but when asked about my pain I reply, "I don't know what you're talking about."

2. Anger loves the word hate. It tastes sweet in my mouth but it burns on the way down. It says, "I hate what you've done. I hate that I love you. I hate myself for all of this. I hate that we can't go back. I hate that I have to keep going."

3. My bargaining sounds like, "I'll let it go, I can let go. I can pretend just please don't leave. I'll do anything."

4. My depression like the scratchy sweater I've had for six years, ugly and worn out. I slide into it easily though it's rough with my skin. I do not feel good in it but what I once knew as discomfort feels normal now.

5. Acceptance meets me quietly. It does not storm the castle. It does not burn my pain to the ground. It meets me right where I'm at. It does not make a show of it. It is what it is. Some would rather call it peace. It settles over me gently reminding me that I'm okay and when I am not I will be again soon.

I am 12, I am 19, I am 23,
Passing through each stage
Just to start over again.
I start over.
It's okay to start over.
I write myself a letter for the next time.
It reads, "You have to face the pain eventually.
It's okay to give it time.
It's okay to wait,
but as soon as you are ready
you have to face the truth.
Yes, it will hurt but I promise
it's a battle worth surviving.
It's okay to hate for a little while
just make sure it's not for too long.

It will hurt you more than they did.
Don't waste your heart on hate.
It's okay to love someone anyway,
but don't love yourself less.
'No matter what' is not always the right thing for you.
It's not right to love someone so much more than yourself
that you would let them hurting you become a habit.
It's okay to be sad,
the kind of sadness that gets inside your bones.
I promise it won't break you.
You are so much stronger than you give yourself credit for.
You have to keep going.
There is so much more life in you.
It's okay to grieve.
It's okay to start the process over.
It's okay if the order switches up on you.
It's okay to stay in one stage longer than another.
It's okay to stay for a little while.
It's okay if that little while takes longer than expected.
It's okay if it takes a few days
or much, much longer.
Don't rush yourself.
Stop rushing yourself.
It's okay to mourn for every type of loss,
for people, for friendships, for love, for jobs,
for health, for faith, for dreams,
and the way you used to be.
It's okay to grieve for any type of change.
It's okay to grieve for yourself.
You may start over,
but it's okay to start over.
It's okay. You're okay.
And when you're not
you will be again soon."

Gone But Not Forgotten

I miss you
and I think that's okay.
I think it's okay to miss the person you once were.
I mourn for the before and not the after.
I remember you before the selfish parts bled into the good,
before you swallowed the hate whole
and spit out every bit of love that could have saved you.
I remember my young hands,
nails poorly painted pink
rolling down the Mustang's windows.
I lean out to taste the ocean's salt in the air.
I asked when you were gonna teach me how to drive.
You said, "Someday baby, soon enough."
There was a time when we never pictured a future
where we wouldn't be together.
I remember the way you laughed whenever you got nervous.
Daddy, I do that too.
How can I laugh and not think of you?
I want to remember how I felt
when you first asked me to pick a book to read to you.
I underlined each letter
with those pink chipped fingernails.
I sounded out every word
through two missing front teeth.
I looked to you for guidance at the start of every sentence.
"Baby, you're doing just fine.
Take your time.
We have plenty of time."
I want to forget how it felt
when you started rushing me as I stumbled over new words.
How you asked me to pick a shorter story next time.
How you started lying whenever you'd tell me,
"Later baby, we'll read later"
I want to forget how I always believed you.
I miss you even when it hurts
because it wasn't always painful to love you.
You taught me to enjoy riding a bike
even when I'm afraid of falling.
but I also learned I can survive most anything
because you're self-absorbed sins didn't break me.

This was a traumatizing lesson.
I deserve to get something out of this.
So I'm keeping the good memories for myself.
I taste the chocolate roses on my birthday.
I woke up to them every year.
I can hear our puppy barking.
You let me choose her name.
I smell the mango tree in our backyard.
You showed me how to climb it.
I remind myself it's okay
to miss the before and not the after.

Barbara

I don't remember much about my father's mother
except that I was her only granddaughter
and she'd tell me I was her favorite anyway.
She'd tell me I was her favorite kind of bird,
tiny but resilient.
She was the flower that fed me sweet promises like,
"I will always love you."
She showed me what unconditional love looked like.
It looks like her heart breaking for me
and for her son.
She had such little time left here with us
but she used it to love so bravely
that the unforgiveable became forgivable.
I think of God's love when I remember her.
I think of hummingbirds
and how they shouldn't be able to fly,
but the impossible
becomes possible
every single day.

Celeste

I don't remember much about my grandmother
except that she gave her daughter a face to match her own
and taught her to make a home for prayers on her lips.
She spoke to God
and God spoke through her.
She taught my mother what it means to intercede.
How to pray for people
when they're not ready
to pray for themselves.
How to pray for your daughter
when she's not ready
to pray for herself.
My mother's prayers for me
are her mother's prayers for her reborn.
I get to know her through knowing my mother.
I hope to resemble them both someday.
My grandmother saw angels
and I saw faith personified.
It has been passed down
through the generations to me.
Prayers are making themselves at home on my lips.
I have my grandmother's smile.

Practice Makes Forgiveness

I have trained for the marathon that is forgiving myself.
I have the stamina.
I have my master's degree in teaching you how to do the same
but it still pains me to forgive those who are not sorry,
as if God hasn't spent years doing the same for me,
but more than anything
I hate forgiving the people who hurt the ones I love so deeply.
I hold a grudge
like a mountain climber without a harness,
their fingers strong and bloody,
holding on for life.
Like an owner's hands
on an anxious dog's leash,
so afraid to let it go.
Like a big sister's grip
on her baby brother's hand
as they cross the busy street.
Like a search party clings to their flashlights,
refusing to give up
even when the batteries begin to die.
I want to pry my fingers off,
to let it fall out of my grasp.
I want a black belt in this,
I want a trophy case,
I want to set a record.
I want to be known for this.
I want to practice every day.

Let It Go

I know you'll never read this.
So, I guess I'm free to say whatever I want,
whatever my heart needs,
but the only thing pouring out of me is:
I miss you.
I admired you for years.
I tore myself apart to emulate your healthy mind,
your ambitious attitude.
I was losing pieces of myself
not realizing you were gathering them up behind me
to throw in my face eventually.
I defended you, I protected you,
I forgave you, I accepted you.
I took care of you the best I could,
like a best friend should,
but I didn't notice when you started to grow a hate for me.
I didn't realize until it was too late.
You locked the door and swallowed the key.
I don't know what I could have done differently.
I don't know who you are anymore.
I don't know how you are anymore.
I don't know if you felt safe enough to cry to anyone
when your grandma died.
I don't know if you ever feel lonely or tired or scared
or if I could have helped
if I had only been there.
All I'm trying to say is, I care.
I never stopped caring even when you
stopped wanting to take care of me in return.
But writing this makes me think
about my place in this world
and how it's not to be a part of yours anymore.
Not if it hurts.
Life can be painful enough
I don't need love that hurts.
I need to let it go. I've gotta let you go.
I don't regret any of it. I hope you know that.
I think of you and mostly smile.
I keep the good memories close.
I let the pain go.

Sticks & Stones

It's been years now
but sometimes I think my clothes
still smell like your house.
I breathe in memories.
I don't remember everything you said
but I remember fearing your words were gonna break me.
I remember sticking up for myself on your stone driveway,
raindrops freckling my skin,
and thinking how cruel it is
that words have always had a way
of hurting me so deeply;
so much more than any physical injury.
Now that I write poetry
I use pain as inspiration.
Sometimes my sweaters smell like you,
and my bones still ache when it rains,
but now your words only help
to create beautiful things.

Heart Of A Warrior

I want to dismantle my belief
that sensitivity is a weakness
I am forced to carry.
I've heard that for so long
I started to agree.
But I reject that,
I shun it.
To be gentle is to be brave.
I use compassion as a weapon.
I strap it to my back.
I could not bear its weight
if I was spineless.
I fight for what is right.
I advocate.
I speak the truth.
I want justice and equality.
I want to play a part in ending stigma.
I will not be ashamed of my heart any longer.
It is capable of so much empathy.
That is a sign of strength.
I will carry it proudly.

People Are Not Burdens

You admit, "They make me feel like a burden."
I feel like all the air has left the room.
How could anyone dare to do this to you?
I am 25 and I live with my mother.
Sometimes, for whatever reasons,
I am too anxious to pump gas.
I start to panic.
How will I get to work in the morning?
What is wrong with me?
Why can't I get it together?
My mother will leave her bed at night,
drive my car on E to the closest gas station, and fill it up.
She brings it back to me no questions asked.
She thinks I've fought enough for one day.
She thinks I shouldn't have to explain myself anymore tonight.
She thinks taking care of me
is a privilege
not a duty.
I think everyone should have her heart.
I'm sorry they don't.
I'm sorry they make you feel like you're a chore
they can't wait to be done with.
No one deserves to feel like something to be checked off a list.
I know a child that may never speak a word out loud.
Let's call her Emma.
She has a best friend.
Let's call her Stella.
Stella is almost always talking,
especially to Emma.
She never gives up when her questions are not answered,
when she hears no response to her silly stories.
She doesn't move onto a friend that's easier to play with,
someone who will tell her jokes,
confide secrets,
make promises,
she whispers,
"I love you, I love you, I love you,"
in Emma's ear.
Her best friend smiles in return;
that is enough for her.

Their friendship is not a burden
for Stella to carry,
for Emma to apologize for.
Emma is not a ball and chain.
She is not a punishment or dead weight.
She is worthy of love
regardless of what she can say.
She is enough, enough, enough.
You are enough;
even if you're not moving on at the pace they prefer,
even if you take up more space than expected,
even if you come with baggage, and limitations.
There should not be a time limit on their compassion for you.
Their support should not run out.
You are not a burden;
you are a person,
a beautiful living thing.
You are enough,
you are a gift,
you are worthy.
I will say it again and again.
When I'm with you
these words are the only things I am carrying.

Unconditional

I've met your bad side.
I've seen all the parts of you
that you were afraid would make me run away.
When someone needed your help
I've seen you think of yourself first.
I've seen the way you lose your patience when you're tired
and I've seen you exhausted.
I've seen the way you can lie
when accepting an apology.
You grow resentment like weeds
choking the life out of a garden
where forgiveness could have blossomed.
You hold a secret grudge.
I've seen the way it eats away at you.
I've seen you at your worst,
the anger taking over,
the fear keeping a hold of you.
I've seen how many times you've wanted to give up
but I choose you anyway.
I want all of you.
I'm not scared to love you on the hard days.
You are so much more than your flaws.
You are so much more than your mistakes.
My love comes with grace.
When you aren't feeling like yourself
I look into your eyes
and I still recognize you.
I lay my head on your chest.
I listen close to each familiar beat.
I know your heart well.
I know you well.
I accept you completely.
I choose every single piece of you,
the ugly and the beautiful.
My love comes with compassion.
It is empathetic.
I want to live on your good side.
The weather there is lovely,
but if it starts to rain
I will travel to the other side.

The storm is getting pretty bad here,
but I know you're scared to be alone
so I'm prepared to stay awhile,
as long as it takes.
I know exactly what I'm getting into.
I won't abandon any part of you.
I'm choosing all of you.
My love for you is unconditional.

Road Trips & Hot Chocolate

I know sometimes you forget
I have more than one role.
I am more than the person
who will take care of you
when you're lonely, sad or drunk.
I am proud that the vulnerable trust me,
that I'm considered strong enough
to face their pain head on.
There is so much honor in that,
but please try and remember
it's not the only part I can play.
Come find me
when they add the newest season of Bob's Burgers to Hulu
and you want to watch it all the way through.
Lean on me when you're thinking about leaving him,
when she wants to see other people again,
but call me just to get coffee too.
Remember I don't drink coffee
and take me some place where they make really good hot chocolate.
It is a sacred thing that you would come to me
holding all your broken pieces
asking me to make something beautiful out of you.
I stitch you back together the best I can.
I knot the thread with hope.
It is a privilege to help you heal.
Just don't forget to call when things feel better.
They will feel better soon,
and when that day comes and you're looking for someone
to co-pilot your next road trip,
think of me.
I'll bring the snacks and a kickass playlist;
some tissues if you really do need to vent.
Just don't forget I have more than one side.
I can sing more than one note.
I have my place,
just remember it's not only by your side
on the hard days.

Cira in Chicago
Summer 2017

Mosaics Too Are Beautiful

You keep talking like you're broken
in this absolute way;
like you have damage
that love cannot repair,
that God cannot reach.
You talk about heart break
and I know it's a figurative term,
but no matter which way we put it
your heart is the strongest muscle in your body.
It is not weak enough to permanently shatter.
You are resilient.
You always make a comeback.
I've watched it firsthand.
I'm not saying the recovery is easy.
I'm just saying you always find a way to mend the break.
I know you're tired
of people taking advantage of your heart
and its place on your sleeve;
as if its vulnerability
was a sign of weakness
and not bravery,
but I think it's right where it belongs.
It is a courageous thing to love so fiercely
that you would keep your heart out in the open
always prepared to try again.
It is a badge of honor.
You have earned it.
Wear it with pride.
Your heart is a survivor.
I know you're so tired of begging for help
to put it back together as you watch it fall apart
in someone else's hands.
Maybe they were young and careless,
a baseball through the window.
Maybe they knew better
but thought only of themselves,
a hit and run.
I will help you patch the holes.
I will apply pressure
until you are ready to clot on your own.

Your pieces will reach for each other
until they fill in the gap.
I will reach for you until I fill the gap.
I will not let the defeat spread with every beat.
You and I will put you back together.
We will fill each crack with gold.
You will resemble the stained glass
in a church's windows.
You will look different but
mosaics too are beautiful.

Hope Will Know My Name

I am surrounded by loved ones
but depression drags me to an empty room.
It is patient as it waits for me to forget
that there is anybody looking for me.
It leans in close and whispers lies like,
"They don't believe your pain is real
or maybe they haven't even noticed it.
But they have noticed you're not fun anymore,
that they don't miss you
like they thought they would.
They don't miss you
like you thought they would."
Depression has started a fight and wants me to believe
I have nobody in my corner.
So it isolates me.
It locks the door,
hangs a sign upon the handle that reads,
"Do not disturb."
It draws the blinds.
Just long enough for its lies to crawl into my ear
and make themselves comfortable
so that when I am found,
when my loved ones lead me out,
I no longer trust them.
Depression asks me, "Why didn't they find you sooner?
Did they even look?
They would never understand.
You could never make them understand.
They'll judge you.
They already judge you."
I am surrounded by loved ones
but I feel so alone in this.
Depression says, "This is going exactly according to plan."
But my loved ones, they have plans too.
They find me when I get lost in this pain.
They keep promises.
They check in.
They ask how I'm feeling
and they want to know the truth.
They take care of me

and sometimes that's picking up my prescriptions
and sometimes it's just listening.
Sometimes it's lying in the dirt with me
as I dig my hands into the earth
and beg for my perception of things
to be grounded in reality.
I plead for paranoia and its older sister anxiety
to forget my name.
I ask my fears to let me go.
They ask my fears to let me go.
They fight for me.
Sometimes we just exist together.
When my pain is too great for any words
they just show up.
when there are no right words to say
They stay anyway.
They breathe the same air as I do.
They mourn beside me.
We don't even have to touch.
I will still feel that they are there.
This is what it means to be here for someone.
Depression falls to its knees pleading with me to walk away,
to follow it back into its room.
Its whispers become shouts.
It yells, "They don't really love you.
They'll give up on you as soon as they get the—."
I cut it off. I interrupt.
I say, "I could really use a friend right now."
I am surrounded by loved ones.
They hear me.
They listen.
They answer,
"You don't ever have to feel alone."

Difficult To Believe; Extraordinary

I look up other words for incredible
because I want to broaden my vocabulary for you.
I want to describe you well.
Wonderful, remarkable, spectacular.
You are an epiphany.
I never realized how proud I could be
until I called you my friend.
I want to bring you peace,
like my mother brought me roses
after the only boy that I ever tried to love
stopped trying to love me.
He had never brought me flowers.
I want to defend you like my best friend in 5th grade
when the bullies made fun of me;
a nail-polish-painted steel combat boot
to the shin of your enemies.
I think your greatest nemesis is anxiety.
I want to beat it to a pulp,
defend your honor,
make you realize you are worth fighting for.
I want you to trust me even when it's frightening,
a rock climber and her harness.
I love you like a child loves a firefly.
I want to hold you close
and set you free.
You light up the whole sky.
I stare in awe of all your beauty.

You Are Not Alone In This

I know you just want be alone
but that won't stop me from being here for you.
I can't sit back and watch you isolate yourself.
I hate the thought of you being lonely in your pain.
I will plant myself outside the walls that you have built
to keep yourself from getting too close, from being let down.
I will rise up like an oak tree.
I hope to bring you shade when you are burning.
I will grow taller than your fortress.
My branches reach out for you over your highest walls.
You have lived for years inside a jail cell
that you have built around yourself
but it never feels like home.
I will help you find the way out.
It gets closer every minute.
You are the lone captain putting on a brave face
when you're afraid you've been abandoned.
You will go down with your ship,
but I am your anchor,
strong and secure.
I've been here all along.
I will meet you at the bottom of the sea.
You don't have to be alone.
I am here for you.
I am a place to be yourself at.
You can feel at home with me.
I will remind you to forgive yourself.
I will teach you how to grieve.
I am in the trenches.
I am a storm chaser.
I am a compass.
I am the phone picking up your call at 3 in the morning.
I will shower you with grace until the shame has rinsed away.
I will stay.
I'm not sure I can save you from yourself by being here for you,
but it won't be for lack of trying.

Sincerely Yours

I want to be your caretaker
because all I want do is help you.
I want to be your bodyguard
and protect you from yourself.
I want to listen to my loved ones
and paint a portrait of what they see in me.
I want to do the same for you.
We don't see the truth in a mirror;
we can't see a reflection of our hearts.
I think our paintings would be beautiful
but I'm just a poet and all I've got are my words.
They are messages in bottles.
I cast them out into the sea.
The waves bring them back to me
when I feel stranded and alone.
They tell me it's okay to tell the truth,
it's okay to ask for help,
it's okay to not be better yet,
it's okay if you need more time.
Give yourself time.
It's okay to lean on others.
It's okay to share the weight.
So when my poetry has finished taking care of me
I return it to the sea
in hopes it would wash onto your shore
and you would find it comforting.
I use my words as a map
for me to follow when I'm hurting.
I uncover hope buried at the end.
I will give you directions.
I will lead the way.
I will carry you if you grow weary.
My poems are love letters.
They remind me to be patient with myself
and to be kind to others.
I hope they can do the same for you.
I want to write something
that would speak to you so loudly
it would silence any words
that was ever used to hurt you.

I know they repeat themselves
over and over again in your head.
I want to shout over them.
I want to be the hand that picks you up
and dusts you off.
I want to wipe away your tears,
pat you on the back,
hold your hand tightly when it's shaking.
I want to be your participation trophy.
You deserve something for trying so hard,
for giving your all.
I want to be salve on your skin.
I want soothe your pain
when you are aching to find relief.
The world has strung together words on to a bow
to use against us
but I believe that poetry
and all its honesty can heal the wounds they left behind.
They try and tell us that pain is a private matter,
that we should be ashamed of ourselves,
that our voices don't need to be heard,
and I'm just a poet, but remember
it's amazing what we can do with our words.

A Sigh Of Relief

Your love reminds me
I can keep going,
that I should keep going.
I have so much to remind me of that
but sometimes
that feels distant or untrue.
So I find myself sinking into the earth,
being swallowed by the quicksand,
overwhelmed by the darkness,
haunted by the loneliness.
forgetting how to breathe,
weighted down from fear,
shoes made from cement,
buried by hopelessness,
a gift from depression.
Your love reminds me
to fight to reach the air,
to burst out of the ground.
You take my hands,
you pull me out.
I gasp like a newborn
tasting air for the very first time.
I cling to oxygen.
It feels precious now.
Your love reminds me
to gather it in my lungs,
to breathe it in
and let it out
even when it aches,
especially when it aches,
even when I have to demand myself to do it.
You remind my lungs to move.
You tell me to be greedy
with every breath,
to save some for later,
to hoard it,
savor it,
be grateful for it.
You remind me
that I have so much here to fight for.

Loving you feels effortless
and so little feels that way lately.
Loving you feels soothing.
It feels simple.
It's a relief.
It feels natural.
It feels like my body knowing how to breathe
without every needing reminding.
It feels like both feet planted on stable ground,
the way it should be.
I promise to do the same for you,
to love you just as deeply.
I promise my love
will keep you far from hopelessness' reach.
I will remind you how to breathe.

Take Hold

I cross the border. I see the big blue sign.
I am welcomed to Michigan.
I have so many good memories here but
that was before.
That was before your family stopped trying to love me,
that was before you made me someone difficult to love,
that was before they chose you,
that was before the cancer took your mother.
You know she never would have let this happen.
She never would have let me go.
She would have chosen us both.
That's all I really wanted.
I never wanted to keep their love from you.
I still loved you back then too.
I just wanted to be cherished, chosen, kept.
Did you have any idea how much you'd take from me?
My brain was getting sicker every day.
I was plagued by fear.
I wanted to visit my family
but I would have brought it on the trip with me,
a carry on.
I'd leave its residue staining the walls of their homes,
a haunting.
I didn't want to scare them.
I didn't want to keep carrying around the guilt
of breaking our family.
I was so young and my arms were so tired.
You should have taken it all upon yourself
but I wish they had at least offered to share the weight with me
when you didn't.
I know that it was hard to be there for me.
I know caring for me didn't come easy
but in hindsight I see that
I deserved the effort.
I am still worthy;
fragile and damaged,
I am still worthy of love.
I don't even know if you talk to them anymore.
I don't know if they call you on your birthday
or save a seat for you on Thanksgiving every year.

Maybe they forgot about you too.
You're pretty hard to love yourself.
Maybe they didn't choose either of us.
Maybe I didn't ask loud enough
but I was just a little girl.
I shouldn't have had to raise my voice
to get your family,
my family,
our family,
to show they care.
I shouldn't have had to beg.
They should have tried harder.
I never did anything deserving of you
taking my family from me.
I refuse to take the blame.
If I could, I would tell your father,
"It wasn't my sins that broke your wife's heart
in the last days of her life.
That guilt belongs to your son."
The loss doesn't hurt like it used to.
I made a new family.
They don't turn away
even when it's painful to watch me suffer.
They love me regardless of my mental illness
and how difficult it makes caring for me.
They put in a lot of effort.
They remind me that I deserve it.
I smile as I see the welcome sign.
One of my closest friends is behind the wheel.
She makes me feel at home wherever we go.
We are on the way to see some of our favorite people.
One of our best friends
will sing some of our favorite songs
and we plan to sing along.
I'm gonna hear my dear friend,
my favorite poet,
pour his heart out
screaming my favorite poems
about my only Father that matters.
Maybe I'll let some of my heart slip out too.
I might share a poem of my own.
My best friends make me feel brave enough to.

We are here to make more memories.
The kind that'll keep us warm at night
when the Michigan winter creeps under our covers.
These memories will wrap themselves around me
and never let me go like the Badens did.
There is so much for me to hold onto from Michigan;
memories of the first time I saw snow as a kid,
uncle David's log cabin,
going for a ride in Grandpa's little yellow airplane,
hummingbirds, tea parties, the grapes,
the magic kingdom
that was really just a backyard.
I will never forget my grandmother sitting at her desk,
hand sewing my baby doll's clothes.
I will remember Tina's laugh filling the car,
Dan believing in me enough to share his stage with me,
every time Chris reminded me that
God deserves all the glory.
There is so much for me to hold onto from Michigan,
new and old
so I'm letting your family go.

Take Hold Fest 2017

Ok, Cupid

Your heart aching to love
and be loved
does not define you.
I know that love will find you
with perfect timing.
Now is your chance to grow into yourself.
It's your time to bloom,
to become who you really are.
Try a couple versions on,
see which one fits right.
You could meet the one,
the love of your life,
the person you want to grow old beside
tomorrow
or maybe in 6 months or 8
but what if it takes 3 years?
Or 10? Or 20?
What if you're already old when you meet?
I'm writing you this poem to remind you that
your value does not decrease every moment you spend alone.
If your wedding day is a week after you turn 53
that is okay.
Your love is young
even if you are not anymore.
It is precious and new,
it is everything you wanted.
It was worth the wait,
the stigma and the loneliness
because a great wife will not be the only thing
etched into your gravestone,
written in your obituary.
There will be so much more to say in your eulogy.
I don't want to trivialize your dreams
or mock your capacity to love, your craving for it,
or sweep your loneliness under the rug.
I just want to remind you
that there is so much more to you than that.
It's a brave and beautiful thing
to be someone's spouse,
to be someone's everything,

to come home to love every day
but I will forever be able to describe you
without saying his name.
I will talk of the ways you helped so many foster kids,
how you never gave up on them,
how often you became a home to them.
I'll speak about your laugh
and how contagious it is,
especially in the bleak and somber moments.
Your laughter spreads quickly, it spreads fiercely.
It is needed like water in a forest fire.
I could soak in it for days.
I'll tell people how you turned your pain into poetry,
how you are making your mark,
leaving fingerprints
on every person who reads it.
Proving to us all
that this incredible, messy world
is better for having you in it.
I will give a beautiful speech at your wedding
and until then I'll write you a thousand poems.

If My Words Spoke As Loud As My Actions

I laugh at a cruel joke.
Regret creeps up my neck.
Why did I think that was funny?
I carry this question the rest of the day.
I try to fall asleep with it settling
in the back of my mind
but a nightmare wakes me.
My fear is what if every word
that I ever created
came alive and followed me?
Would they be ugly?
Something I would beg to hide?
Would they scare me?
Would I pretend to not see them standing there?
Would they try to hurt me?
Or would they go after the people around me?
Would I be ashamed to introduce them?
Would I want them to be popular?
Would I be proud
to let them walk beside me?
I'm afraid not.
and that embarrasses me.
There are so many things
language can create,
poetry, lyrics, scripts,
recipes, love letters,
get well soon and birthday
and anniversary
and thank you cards,
graduation invitations,
a powerful story,
a best man's speech,
a moving eulogy,
instructions, directions, captions,
letters of recommendations,
compliments,
and apologies.
I don't want to waste my voice
creating monsters.
If my words were personified

I'd want them to be the doctor
who holds the daughter
of the man newly diagnosed with dementia
as she weeps into their white coat.
She is not their patient
but they take care of her anyway.
I'd want them to be the mother
who looks into her infant's blind eyes
and sees a perfect baby.
I'd want them to resemble Jesus
when He said, "Forgive them Father,
they know not what they do."
I'd want my words
to look like the social worker
that replaces trash bags
with a suitcase.
I'd want them to be the photographer
that sheds a tear themselves
as they capture the groom sobbing
at the sight of his bride
walking towards him.
I'd want them to be a counselor,
a pastor,
an artist,
an activist,
a teacher,
a friend,
someone I am proud to be seen with,
someone I am not ashamed to name.
I'd want them to be
someone that speaks up for what is right,
encourages those in pain,.
I want my voice to only create
kind, gentle, beautiful things.

I Don't Want To Be A Thorn In Your Side Anymore

I cut my mother with my thorns
and she still thinks I'm the most beautiful rose she's ever seen
but that doesn't keep responsibility from me.
I hurt her when I'm hurting,
like a scared dog biting the owner who once
rescued it,
wanted it,
chose it;
like a house crumbling in a storm,
burying the people who restored it years ago,
made it beautiful,
made into a home.
I pride myself on honesty
but I haven't been telling the whole truth.
I write a lot about depression and its hopelessness,
the shame and isolation-
but the mania, I keep those stories to myself.
The way anxiety brings out all the selfish parts of me,
I don't like to share that side of the story.
These things have me choosing fight over flight
more often than I want to admit.
I've kicked others while they were already down
but I don't like to talk about it.
I regret it, resent it,
I want to deny it
but I don't think it's something
I can keep pretending isn't happening.
I write poems about taking care of one another,
about being gentle with each other's hearts.
I want to teach people about empathy
but I can't ever stop practicing what I preach.
I am not better than anyone else.
I am still learning.
I'm still screwing up.
I let my best friends down.
I say I'll always be there
but I don't always stick around.
I retreat into myself.
My pain becomes more important to me than anything else,
than anyone else

and for that I am so sorry.
I'm still trying to control my self-righteous attitude.
I carve out the judgmental corner of my heart,
toss it down the basement stairs,
throw away the key
but it grows back,
like it belongs there.
I don't want it take root and spread.
I'm doing my best
but there are so many moments
when that is not enough.
I need to own that.
I lose my patience with my students.
I have given up on people.
I can be two-faced, a gossip,
I haven't always kept secrets.
I let my mood disorder control me.
I go into battle against it
and I don't care if there are casualties.
My allies would die beside me
and sometimes I forget to even thank them.
I have seen what I am capable of
and it scares me.
I keep forgiveness from those who hurt my loved ones,
as if they deserve grace any less than I do.
I tell God He deserves no credit for my victories.
I make my mother walk on eggshells,
hot coals, a bed of my thorns
as if she controls the exhausting,
terrifying, inconsistency inside of me.
As if this chronic pain is somehow her fault,
as if she cracked open my skull
and planted this disease.
Mom, I am sorry.
I want to do better.
I want to be better.
I want to treat you
and everybody else better.
I accept responsibility.
I want to be held accountable
even if it includes this kind of honesty,
telling the world that I can be so damn ugly,

quick to anger,
quicker to deny any culpability.
I want to be faster in my apologies.
I don't want them to feel familiar.
I don't want them to be needed this often.
I want them to be honest.
I want them to be rare.
I want them to sound like, "I'm sorry I hurt you"
and feel like a promise
to be more careful,
to show more restraint.
I want to trim my thorns.
I want you to be able to hold me without flinching.
I want to be the most beautiful rose you've ever seen.

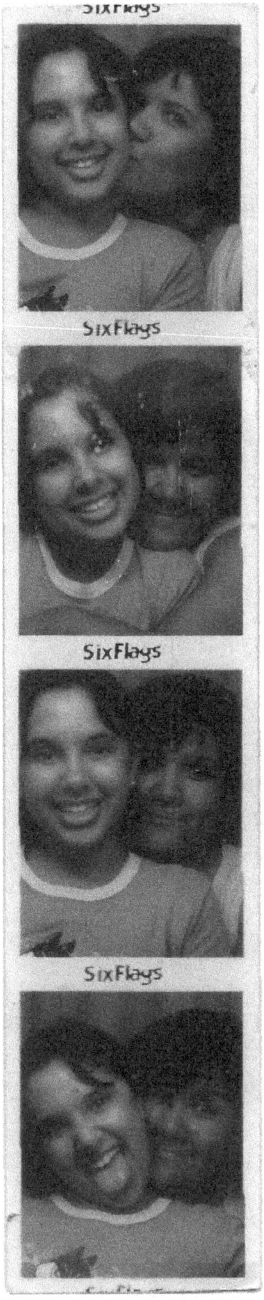
SixFlags
SixFlags
SixFlags

The Great Quake Of 2018

I don't want to forget
to check in on people,
the day after,
the week after,
6 years after.
Time has its way of healing us
but it doesn't always look linear.
It's not the same as erasing,
it is not a smooth ride,
an easy process.
There is turbulence.
Your stitches rip
and the wounds reopen;
sometimes we tear them out ourselves.
It's the hardest thing you've ever done
and you will still feel like
you should just get over it.
There are anniversaries every year,
we apply for a new job
knowing they'll ask why we left the last one
so abruptly,
we sleep alone for the first time in years,
we flinch at the slightest touch,
the insurance doesn't cover the new treatment,
we replace the flowers on gravestones,
nothing was saved in the fire,
there's no baby coming home from the hospital with us,
we start failing our classes,
we have a harder time getting out of bed,
we start skipping meals again.
In times like these people too often give you space,
too much space
after they shave their head for you,
their hair grows back
and your phone doesn't ring as often.
There's too much space
after the 4th time you've gotten out of rehab,
the 3rd miscarriage,
the 2nd eviction notice,
or the month after you tried to kill yourself.

Maybe this isn't the first time
you've mentioned divorce,
or slept in your car for a couple of weeks,
or moved far, far away.
Maybe you've been sick for a very long time.
Maybe they don't take you seriously enough
or maybe they're just giving you too much space
like after you've eaten all the casseroles
and replied to all the condolences
and the quiet sounds so loud.
You sign the papers,
they throw you a party
but no one thinks to call you
on Valentine's day.
We forget to ask you if you need help
donating your dress.
We don't even notice
when you go back to your old name.
People are flawed;
we forget,
we are selfish,
we get busy,
we don't make time,
we don't know what to say,
we don't want to say the wrong thing,
so we don't say anything at all.
We think skipping the subject
might bring you relief.
I'm sorry that you're not alone
but you feel so lonely.
I'm sorry I forgot
it would have been your brother's birthday.
You'll never forget.
The least I could do is remember with you.
I'm sorry I didn't check on you
after that argument with your girlfriend.
I knew it was a bad one but I figured you would reach out
if you needed anything,
but sometimes it's hard to reach out
when you feel like all your bones are breaking.
I'm sorry that I let so much time grow
between my 'how are you's.

I'm sorry that when it was hard to be there for you,
I wasn't.
I'm sorry for not calling you back,
for not calling you first.
I want my heart to set an alarm,
mark the calendar.
I don't want you to feel lost
and forgotten
in all the space I'm giving you.
I want to be there through it all.
The earthquake,
the aftershock,
the relief efforts,
the rebuilding of your city,
I want to donate my time
and my love.
When we look at your history books
of the aftermath of the great quake of 2018
I want to be in every picture.

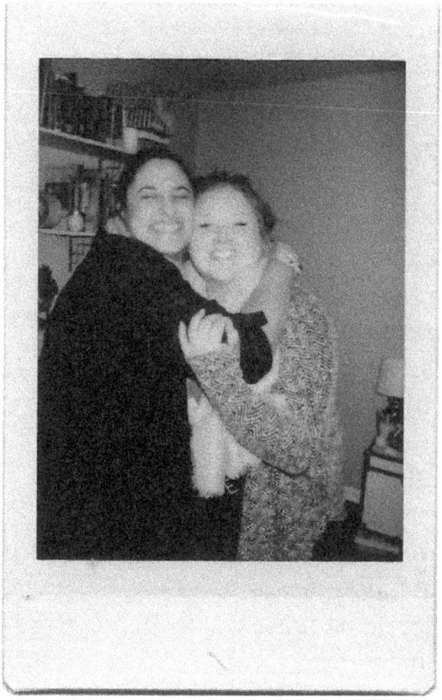

The Valley

More hope is on its way.
It'll be here any minute
but we don't have to wait.
We don't have to stay.
We can leave right now.
I've come to get you out of here.
This poem is for the people waiting for things to get better.
The kind who say, "The lines here always take forever
I may as well sit down."
I'm here to tell you to stay on your feet.
It's time to leave.
This poem is for the people rationing their hope;
Not knowing for sure things will ever get better again,
but willing to wait to find out.
They are lacking hope, full of doubt;
this poem says pack your shit we're leaving.
We don't need absolute confidence.
We don't need promises or proof first.
We just need a shred of hope;
a maybe, a what if, any bit will do.
We are getting out of this place.
We're gonna find where you belong.
I know what you're thinking.
No, it's not perfect out there,
but we aren't looking for a paradise or any cures.
We understand the ebb and flow
and whenever we forget, we can remind each other.
Things get better, and then maybe they get worse.
They take a sharp left and we arrive here once again,
but the next day may be the best one in your whole life.
We may come back here often.
I don't know how to stay away forever.
I don't have all the answers.
All I know is that things can always get better.
As long as there is air in your lungs
and time on your clock,
things can get better again.
Ebb and flow.
This poem is not about getting happy and staying that way.
This poem is not a miracle.

It's assurance that you don't belong here.
This poem is just a spark
but it can burn down the house you are trying to build here.
It's a demand that you stop wallowing in the valley.
This poem is an offer to take the next train out of this place.
It's a reminder that you don't have to dwell here
just because you know your way around.
You were ready to leave a long time ago.
You just weren't sure it was worth it.
Why leave when you know you'll be back here again someday?
Maybe sooner than later.
This poem is for the doubtful, the hopeless,
the ones who are so tired they just stay put.
This poem says it's time leave anyway.
This place is not your home.

Shock Trauma

I think I'm over it. I think it's in the past.
I shut the door behind me
but trauma creeps in closer when I'm not expecting it.
It begins pounding on the doors,
tearing at the seams,
trying to rip its way out of me.
I hear it when my brakes squeak.
I react unexpectedly, unsettled,
there's something about that sound.
The clock turns back
and I see myself as a child
hiding in the bathroom from daddy,
forgetting that the door creaks,
forgetting to lock it behind me.
I feel it when someone reaches out to hold my hand.
My hands are the most sensitive part of my body.
I want to cut them off at the wrist.
I can't stand the feeling of being held sometimes,
even if it's only our palms touching.
When our fingers grasp tight to one another
too often I am suffocating.
Trauma leaves me fragile
so I hang a sign around my neck
that says, "Please, don't touch the glass."
I hear it in the word *relax,*
always in my father's voice.
Not when we're talking about vacations or a nap
but when someone is patronizing me,
trivializing my concerns,
my anxiety,
my intuition telling me
that something isn't right,
something needs to change,
that this is not okay.
I smell the orange peels
my student has laid out in front of him at the lunch table.
The soap my father used came in an orange bottle.
He smelled like citrus every day.
I step away.
I gather myself in the staff bathroom

but as I open the door,
I hear it creak.
Time is healing me.
God gives me more every day
and I am learning to start saying
thank you.
I don't think of my father on his birthday anymore.
Thank you.
One of the most important people in my life
was born on the same day.
Daniel would never cut me open
and demand that I stop bleeding.
Thank you.
When I hear the name Chris
I think of my cousin, I think of celebrities,
I think of one of my best friend.
He would never plant a seed of doubt in my mind
of God's love for me
and leave me overgrown and withering.
I don't see my father's face
at the sound of that name anymore.
Thank you.
I've started sleeping through the quiet.
I don't need the music as often
to drown out my fears of tomorrow.
Thank you.
The silence isn't as frightening as it used to be.
The nightmares are retreating.
They have packed their belongings and are getting out of town.
Thank you.
I've started to reach out for my loved ones' hands
when they are hurting.
When there's nothing more to say
I reach out for them.
I hold them close
even if for now it's only with my hands.
I think that says more than anything.
Thank you.
Time is helping me take control
of the damage trauma left behind in its wake.
Time is teaching me how to put a muzzle on its mouth,
restrain it, master it,

keep its teeth far away from my throat.
Time is molding it into something more comforting.
It takes the fragile sign around my neck
and turns it into one for me to hold at the airport
for when people who hurt
from the same kind of pain as I do
arrive in the valley.
It reads, "I am here for you.
You are not alone in this.
I will help you carry your luggage
but we will be leaving this place soon."
Time is helping me to use the scars
trauma left throughout my body.
I take a picture.
I hang it in a museum.
It shows a story of survival.
It shows how much pain one can endure
and still have victory,
how you can bury someone 6 feet under anguish and shame
and watch as they claw their way out from underneath
all those layers of earth and defeat;
grow into a pine tree,
bring joy to the holidays,
keep a family warm when it is snowing
or maybe become a book of poetry.

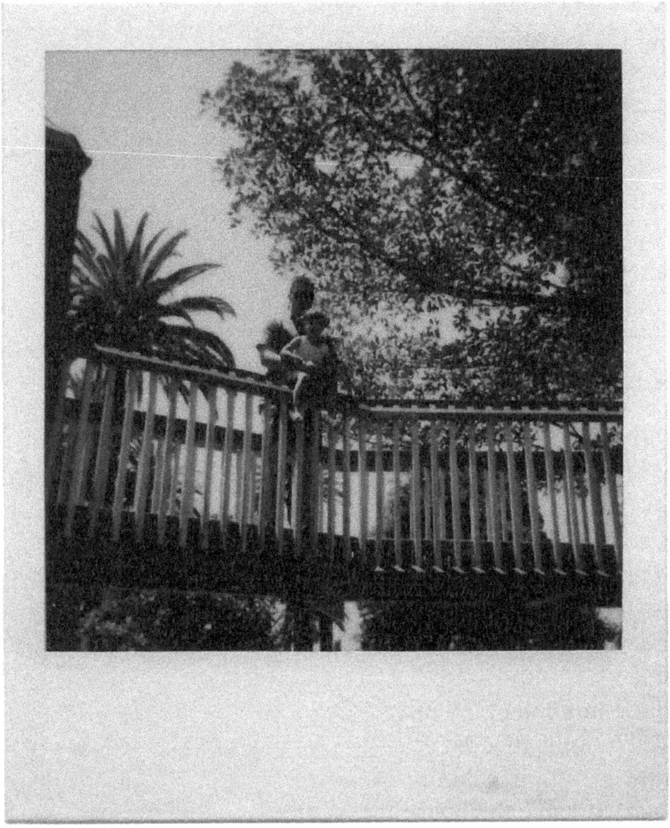

Bittersweet Thank Yous

Every day that I believed you existed
I spent the night dreaming of you.
You were the smallest fraction of a person,
barely a heartbeat,
a maybe, a what if,
but I believed that you were real
so my grief too is real.
And I guess we'll never know for sure
if you were ever really here,
but I am sure that just the thought of your life
being cut short
was enough to save mine.
I owe everything I am
and will ever be to your memory.
I wish I could have saved us both.
I was so scared to ask for help back then,
like riding a bike
or left from right.
I'll always remember how that felt.
I was scared that I was already too damaged,
that at only 16
there was no hope left for me.
I was scared that I was asking for too much.
I was scared of getting better
and I was scared I would always be this way.
I was scared
I was nothing more than my pain.
I swallowed 62 pills that day.
I thought I was saving us both.
It got so hard to leave the house that year.
I was afraid every time I walked through the front door
that it was the last time
I'd be brave enough to leave.
I pushed away my mother
because she would never have given up on me
and I just wanted the freedom
to do so myself.
I felt unsafe in my own skin
so I punished it.
I didn't think that anyone would understand.

I stopped planning for a future.
Didn't think I'd ever be 17
or 18 or 26
or 53.
I didn't think I'd ever know old age.
I didn't think anyone would miss me,
as if I'd never left a mark on anything,
as if my absence wouldn't torture my friends, my family,
all the people who love me,
as if there wasn't anyone
to brush the leaves away from headstone every fall,
as if my mother wouldn't cry for me,
as if my future didn't matter,
as if my pain was greater than God's love for me,
as if suicide had always been my destiny.
I thought loving him might heal me
but I felt betrayed by myself more than anything.
I opened myself up to new pain
because I just wanted to feel something different.
I was tired of the same old ache.
I wanted to see if I pushed myself hard enough
would I reset the bone or would I break?
I thought it was worth the risk.
I ended up with fractures and regret.
I asked him to love me in the all the ways
I needed someone to,
in all the ways I couldn't love myself yet.
He was just a kid and I was asking him to do God's work.
I was pleading for him to erase
every fingerprint that my pain had left on me.
I was asking him to turn back time.
I wanted to be someone new,
someone who cried over ASPCA commercials
and not the one that sheds a tear for every second
she stood alone in the grocery aisle with a man she didn't know.
I wanted to know what it was like to be stressed over homework
and what dress to wear to prom
and not restraining orders,
declining mental health,
and missing someone that almost destroyed you.
I thought I could wear a mask forever
but the nightmares came back

and I found that I couldn't stop being myself.
But if it wasn't for him there would have never been a you,
so I don't regret everything.
Those nightmares started to be replaced by dreams of you.
I thought of all the ways I would protect you,
all the ways I would ensure your safety with my love.
I would never bring out the worst parts of you
like my father did to me.
If your brain had mental illness locked away in it
I would never give you the key.
I would never ask you to love me no matter what.
I would never give you a reason to hate yourself.
But I was sick and I was tired
and I was sick and tired of the healing process.
I was tired of waiting.
I was tired of grieving.
I was tired of not remembering what it felt like
to not feel this way.
I mistook exhaustion for weakness.
I swallowed 62 pills that day
because I thought I had nothing left to fight for.
I thought I had more pain than reasons to stay.
But then I closed my eyes
and dreamed of you.
You would never know
what it feels like to be covered in sand from head to toe,
how to let it scrape away every bad day.
You would never taste my mother's French toast on your birthday.
You would never learn to make bunny ears with laces
or wear a cap and gown.
You would never fall in love with a person
or a job, or a book, or a smell, or a song,
or a moment, or a dream for yourself.
You would never know what it feels like to forgive;
to be hurt so deeply
but to know grace well enough
to share it between yourself and someone else.
You would never know
what it feels like to have an answer to a prayer.
I know that you were the answer to every one
that left my heart that year.
I asked to know that there was more to life than this.

I asked to have a reason so completely undeniable
that I wouldn't have any choice but to keep going.
I asked for something that would keep me here
long enough for me to reach the other side of this.
I asked for hope
that there is another side of this.
It wasn't thoughts of a better future that reached me.
It was the fear of never even giving you a chance to have one.
The image in my mind of your tiny fingers
clinging to my thumb
was the only picture bright enough
for me to see through the darkness that surrounded me.
It opened the door for the thought of my mother
trying to speak at my funeral.
Her pain being too deep for any words.
Her voice would never be the same.
It would always shake when using past tense
and my name in the same sentence.
I could see how what I was doing
would only encourage my best friend
that there was a quicker way out of her pain.
It would tell her giving up was an option,
that hope does not belong to us.
As if it isn't our birthright.
It reminded me that I was 16,
I was only 16.
I was only just starting.
I was still at the beginning
and that thought had always terrified me
but in that moment, I was introduced to hope,
to the idea that I could keep trying,
that I could reach the end of my rope
and tie the cord around my body
to keep myself from falling,
that I had a whole life in front of me
and that finally didn't feel like such a bad thing.
I threw up 62 pills that day.
I counted every one
because I had to be sure I was done
I had to be sure that I was finished giving my future away.
I counted ten for your fingers and ten for your toes,
2 for the years left of high school I would get to finish,

4 for each of my best friends,
5 for every door that was opening for me,
31 for my mother because that was her age when she had me
and I was never gonna make myself be the reason
she would have to mourn for a child.
62 for the 62 years I hoped to have in front of me.
I still find myself dreaming of you.
I'm not sure exactly when I lost you.
I'm not sure your life here ever started
but you saved me from cutting mine short,
and for that I am so thankful.
I only wish I could have saved us both.

2009

I don't understand why two people can experience trauma and only one of them will suffer from mental illness for the rest of their life. I just don't understand. I know the answer is genetics and biology, brain science stuff etc., etc., but it still doesn't make sense to me. It doesn't change the fact that my instinct is to feel jealous when I hear that someone has been through a great amount of emotional pain and walked away from it without chronic mental illness. I feel ashamed that deep down that is my first reaction. It is. I'm just being honest and that's ugly and sad but I'm only human and I'm in pain. It leaves me frustrated... no, it leaves me angry. I feel angry. I feel constantly vulnerable. I feel fragile, as if could probably stub my toe at this point and trigger another anxiety or mood disorder, another disease that I will never be able to cure only "treat the side effects" of. This makes me feel weak and disappointed in myself some days. This makes me feel angry with myself.

We hear all the time that life is unfair, people love to remind me of that but trust me, my life, and my sick brain reminds me of that pretty regularly. And yeah, often times that pisses me off. The hardest part is feeling like it's my fault, that those people that have escaped or avoided chronic mental illness are in some fundamental way stronger than I am; more resilient than I am, more blessed than I am. It makes me feel like the only difference between us is that I am weak and they are not. I have to tell myself every day that that's not true. But honestly? It feels a lot like I'm lying to myself most days. I feel embarrassed when someone applauds me on my strength, like I've been fooling everyone and am about to be caught.

I think that being honest, even if it's sad and ugly like this, I think it's important. I suffered in silence for a long time and I felt like I was the only one who was angry or confused or grieving for the brain I could have had if not for trauma. Maybe my mental illness would have lain dormant, maybe I would have come across different trauma and still gotten here, maybe it would have taken over my brain without any help. I don't know. I'll never know. And yeah, that makes me mad. I'm not saying anger is the right thing or that jealousy feels good because it's not and it doesn't, but that's not my point. My point is that being honest about it, accepting that that's what you're feeling and that you're not alone in that; sharing those feelings even when you're ashamed helps other people know that they're not alone in those same feelings. That's healthy. That's the right thing to do. It makes it easier to loosen your grip on those feelings, to not hold them so close and so damn tight.

If I'm never honest about these feelings and I only preach on how we should never compare our pain to one another, that suffering does not mean we are broken, or weak or failing at the healing process, that we do not deserve blame for having mental illness, if I only ever talk about these things it makes me feel ashamed of doubting them. It makes me feel lonely in my pain. I do doubt them, not when my loved ones are feeling hopeless. I am filled with the need to encourage whenever I see that in someone else's eyes. But when I'm looking into my own in the mirror, sometimes, I have doubts. Sometimes I feel angry, I feel jealous and bitter and broken. If I don't talk about those moments too it only spreads the shame and loneliness.

Life is unfair and sometimes it's even cruel and most of the time it just doesn't make sense. I find comfort in knowing that I'm not alone, that there is still value in my life even if my brain never heals, even if it becomes more damaged. I still have value. God can still use me. There are so many people who grieve for the same things that I do. We are not alone in this. Life is still worth living in spite of all its flaws.

This Poem Is Another Apology

I write a letter to my body.
I say, "I am sorry I didn't tell you this sooner."
This is an apology to my skeleton and its skin,
every joint, every pound, every hair on my head.
I say, "I'm sorry for criticizing you,
for not being gentle,
for not respecting you;
as if we haven't been together for 25 years,
as if you haven't felt my pain; every heart break,
all the guilt, the sorrow and the shame.
I took it out on you
as if you haven't fought for me
in all the battles I have faced,
as if you aren't the temple
I should have worshiped at every single day.
I didn't love you
when that's all you really needed from me."
My letter is longer than I thought it'd be
but I've made so many mistakes.
You deserve a real apology.
I am sorry I didn't tell you this sooner.
I say, "I never should have considered your shape a flaw,
your color a curse,
your skin too damaged.
The marks stretched across your body like tiger stripes,
they are beautiful.
I'm sorry I made you cry
at the thought of someone seeing them.
You should wear them like a badge.
They say this body has learned to adapt.
They match your mother's and your best friend's.
You don't have to be ashamed of them.
I am sorry I didn't tell you this sooner.
I caked your skin in cover-up to hide every blemish
but when that wasn't enough I asked you to hide instead.
It started when you were only 9.
The stress took such a toll on you.
It took me 10 more years
before I let the sun touch your naked face,
your bare shoulders.

I should have never kept that warmth from you.
Now I only compare your scars to paint
being splattered across the canvas of your body.
You are a work of art.
I am sorry I didn't tell you this sooner.
I'm sorry for every time I reminded someone
of your father's pale German skin
asking them to look past the color
your mother passed down to you.
I wanted you to always be labeled as mixed,
diluted, not completely one of her people.
I wanted you to be more acceptable, more relatable
in your small minded town
where people mostly look the same;
mostly nothing like you.
I just wanted you to feel wanted.
I wanted you to feel like you belonged.
I was looking for approval from the wrong people.
They were showing me whiteness was the norm,
the preferred, the privileged.
I wanted you to be less colorful,
but now I promise to admire
the way your skin looks like sand in the wintertime.
I know the ocean feels like home.
I think it's only right you look like you belong there.
In the summer light you are a golden shade of brown.
It is my new favorite color.
It looks like the palm tree trunks that were scattered across
the backyard of your childhood home.
It's the same shade as Lady, the dog you got when you were 4.
She was the prettiest thing you'd ever seen.
It's the way your mother likes her coffee.
I am sorry I didn't tell you this sooner.
You deserve to take up space
regardless of how much you weigh.
Not fitting the mold
does not mean you belong here any less.
They say it's what's on the inside that counts
and that is true
but your body does not need to be erased,
put aside, forgotten, a secret, displaced.
Your thighs are almost always touching one another

like your fingers in a fist,
you are stronger than I gave you credit for.
You carried on even when I introduced you to shame.
I should have explained
that fat is just a descriptor;
it is a fact, not an insult.
Whether other people agree or not,
whether other people like it or not.
That word will no longer be a weapon used against you.
You are 5'8, you have a small gap in your front teeth,
you have brown eyes,
you are fat.
It is not a label for others to read
to decide if they want you or not.
It's just another thing about you
like your love for pineapple on pizza,
your right-handedness, your job title.
I am sorry I didn't tell you this sooner.
I should apologize every day for harming you.
I clawed at your flesh when I was scared
like a cat being thrown into a lake.
I left behind scars laid out like blueprints.
They explain how to punish yourself
for a crime you did not commit.
Forgive me for setting you up.
When I was embarrassed of the marks
I was leaving behind on your skin
I had you lie in bed until your bones ached.
I pulled your hair, I bruised your knuckles on the floor,
I screamed into your pillow at the top of my lungs
until your throat was sore.
I never should have touched you
when I was angry or afraid.
I thought torturing you might give me some answers.
I was wrong.
I was wrong about all of it,
but I'm ready to make things right.
I'm sorry I didn't tell you that sooner."

83

Interwoven Hope

I learned how to braid when I was nine.
I learned what depression felt like soon after.
Years later I would use that knowledge to braid fear into a rope,
wrap it tight around my neck,
always looking for a place to hang it.
But lately hope has begun to unravel it.
replace it with the scarf my mother bought me last fall,
kiss me there like a lover someday will.
It wraps its arms around my neck
like a child saying,
"Thank you for giving me another chance;
I promise you won't regret it."

It's A Shame

If I could crack open each one of my ribs
and rip out the shame from my chest
trust me, I would.
But it would fight for its life
because it's always planned to take mine.
I can't call out for help
because stigma has been building in my heart
from years of choking on the truth
and purging out 'I'm fines'
because I believed the lie
that it's not okay to not be okay this often ,
but I'm done.
A lie, is a lie, is a lie,
no matter how long you believed it,
and the truth is shame has overstayed.
It grew along the walls of my chest like ivy,
strong and defiant,
but it will not make its home here.
As long as my heart is still beating
I have more chances to be honest.
I clear a path from my ribcage to my tongue.
I say, "I am hurting." I say, "I am scared."
I speak the truth
because I don't want my voice to be buried
beneath layers of shame any longer.
I carve away at it every time I say, "It's been hard lately."
I'll keep saying it until asking for help comes out loud and clear.
I want to pay it forward
because my voice has never been as brave
and powerful and beautiful
as when it's asking someone else,
"How are you really doing?"
Honesty pours out of my lips
and sometimes it's used against me
but with every beat,
I try again.

Post-it Notes As A Form Of Coping

I cope as well as I can.
I cope in the only ways I know how.
They work for me.
I cope by writing this poem.
I'll cope by saying it out loud.
I cope by eating Reese's' ice cream
out of the container in Bethany's kitchen
as we watch the Troll's movie
for the hundredth time.
I take medicine.
I stop looking for a cure.
I accept myself.
I cope with dark humor
and big foot documentaries,
by riding roller coasters with my sisters,
our nieces and our nephew,
the family I adopted,
that I want to always belong to.
I cope by talking to God
and my mother
and I am trying to find the right therapist too.
I cope with Wawa egg sandwiches
and going to see Kubo and the Two Strings
by myself.
I come home after a long day of work
and I pour myself a Capri Sun on the rocks.
I drive to Point Lookout
in the middle of the night.
I listen to the waves.
I bring a milkshake
and my mom.
I cope by painting my room,
I hang my art on the walls,
I read TWLOHA's blog.
I cope by trying pizza
in every city I visit.
I listen to Dan's EP on repeat.
I plan out the most perfect Halloween costume
for me and my friends

when it's only June.
We're going with Rocket Power this year.
I wear that big ugly brown sweater.
I get a genie lamp tattoo.
I cope by standing with Ben
in the freezing ocean in September.
I go see my favorite band
and I pretend they played every song
they've ever made.
I text Chris to pray for me
when I'm too discouraged
to do it myself.
I believe God still wants to hear from me
even if it's through somebody else.
I help Brielle move into her new apartment.
She places my first book onto her shelf.
I cope by buying a pineapple - shaped phone case,
then a cactus,
then Baxmax, Totoro,
a chocolate bar,
officer Judy Hopps
and Stitch.
I stand on top of a waterfall.
I've waited years to do this.
My friends brought me here;
they want all my dreams to come true.
Tina and I send each other the same lyrics,
back and forth,
back and forth;
I never grow tired of our song.
I cope by celebrating my birthday
the entire month of February.
I wear a tiara and everything.
I know that's really extra but
I don't always feel like celebrating life.
I think it's important to stretch the party out when I do.
I cope by cutting all my hair off
at 1 in the morning.
I never regret it.
I watch 10 seasons of Survivor
back –to- back with Chelsea.
I lie down on the classroom floor with Josh

when we both feel overwhelmed.
He thinks that's pretty funny,
his laughter really soothes me.
I cope by begging my best friends
to take pictures in the photo booth with me
until they finally give in.
I am always watching for the sunset.
I drop everything
and live out of a car
with my friends for a week
just to hear their songs every night,
to push myself,
because I'm ready to be free.
I laugh loudly,
I laugh often.
I have a worn-out library card
and a favorite spot at the beach.
I keep Kate on speed dial.
I very, very passionately debate Devin
about Kylo Ren being beautiful.
I cry big, ugly, fat tears
over those YouTube videos
of kids finding out they're going to Disneyworld.
I scream Switchfoot's Twenty-Four
as I turn 24.
I cope by checking in on Ciera.
I know that things are tough for her lately.
I find comfort in comforting.
I cope with visualizing
and counting
and breathing techniques
and telling the truth.
I cope with extra sleep.
Yes, Netflix I'm still watching.
I make all the women in my life
handmade valentines
for Galentine's Day.
I wear a lot of yellow,
like school bus,
SpongeBob,
lemon, yellow.
I also wear a lot of floral print

that probably resembles your grandma's couch
because I think it makes me look like sunshine
and a flower garden
and that really makes me smile.
I sing this super cute baby shark song to my students.
I hold them extra tight.
I cope so much better now than I used to.
I was mostly just surviving back then.
I won't spend much time
explaining my alternatives,
my worst-case scenarios.
Sometimes I still fall back on them.
They look like self-injury,
not always in the ways you're used to seeing it.
Sometimes it's just violent words
thrown at the person
who is the most gentle with me.
The shrapnel slices through my body too.
It's skipping my pills
saying, "What's the point if they're not curing me?"
It's refusing to be vulnerable with anybody.
It's isolating myself.
It's holding on to a mantra that just repeats,
"I can't, I can't, I can't."
And yeah, sometimes it cutting;
sometimes it gets physical,
but there are so many more ways to harm yourself.
I've learned that the hard way,
though lately, I've been finding better ways
to wash the pain down.
I chew it up
and swallow it.
The taste is bittersweet.
I am proud of myself
for keeping it down
but I wish it had never crawled in
through my bared front teeth
in the first place.
But I am coping.
I am dealing with it.
I am healing from it
the best I know how.

I cope by putting 8 post-it notes on the wall
I wake up facing every morning.
They say, "You will not always feel this way,
give it more time,
you never would have thought
you would make it this far,
depression is not terminal,
you have so much left to say,
you are still needed here,
keep going,
Janelle, you are loved."

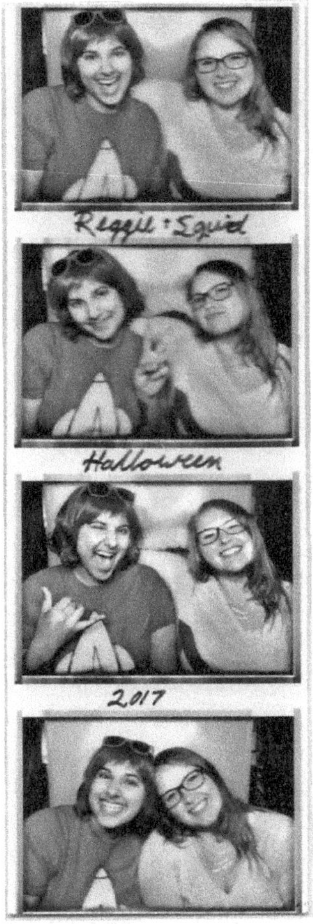
Reggie + Squid
Halloween
2017

This is not the story of a quick recovery but one of a bloody battle; the kind you come out not unscathed but still the victor. It's an invitation to keep trying. It's a promise that it's all worth it. Years ago, when I was 18, I was given an opportunity. Stephen, my youth pastor, invited me to share my testimony, a word of encouragement with a group of my peers in between sets at a show at a local venue. I automatically wanted to say no. It had only been maybe about a year and a half since I had reached my breaking point with my social anxiety. I was becoming housebound. Things were getting really bad but when I hit rock bottom, truly by the grace of God, I decided to get help; started therapy, found the right medication for me, started talking to God again. I found myself eventually in college, getting the right medical treatment, going to church again. I was still suffering, still struggling but I was fighting. I was giving it my all.

Stephen felt God was leading him to invite me to speak. He told me to pray about it but that He really felt like it was God giving me this opportunity. That baffled me. I was honestly angry. I felt betrayed. I felt God should know me better than that. I thought maybe He hadn't been listening to me as much I thought. He should know better than to ask that much of me. But as quickly as the anger came I let it go. I had spent so many years angry with God. I didn't want to grab a hold of that again. It was a lonely and dreadful feeling that I refused to fall back into. If God was pushing me it must be because I could handle it. I wanted to trust Him. I decided I would try. I would go for it. I imagined how good it would feel afterwards. I mean what an underdog story, what a triumph. I had been home schooled for most of my life because of my social anxiety. It was already an incredible feat that I was coming to this youth group. I had been using it as exposure therapy and it was working. Maybe I was ready for this.

I wanted it to work out so badly. I wanted that sense of pride. I wanted to use it as example to encourage other people. I wanted so badly to say that I was proud of myself. In hindsight it breaks my heart I didn't give myself and God more credit than that. I already had so much to be proud of. Every day of my life is a testament to hope and healing. I had come so far. God had brought me so far. I was still hurting so much, fighting every day but I had so much to be proud of myself for.

I would love to tell you I stood on that stage and shared a hopeful story with those people, that I touched someone's life with my words but as Stephen stood there calling my name for me to come up and speak I cried in his wife's arm. I was unable to even make a coherent sentence.

I could barely breathe. Lauren held me. She never tried to guilt or pressure me into going up there. She didn't talk of being obedient to God or sucking it up. She just comforted me. Spoke of God's grace. I wish I had listened closer. I'd like to tell you I felt the presence of God in the room and I marched up there and His words became mine, but that just isn't this story. In that moment I didn't trust God. I doubted Him tremendously. I didn't think He would help me. I felt alone in that moment. He had surrounded me with love and support and I still didn't believe He would comfort me or take away my anxiety. I felt He was asking too much of me. I let that fear consume me and I panicked. I felt defeated. I cried. I felt ashamed. I went home. I was really hard on myself. I spent a long time feeling awful about that night. I felt I had missed an opportunity for a real important step in my recovery. Stephen and Lauren tried to reassure me I would get another chance, that God loved me exactly how I was and no matter what I did or didn't do. I feared there may have been someone there that night who needed to hear my story and didn't. I felt I had let down God, and everyone who had been encouraging me to share my story that night. I couldn't get past those thoughts for a long time.

Fast forward to 2017. I'm 25 and things are very different, but some are still very much the same. I've made huge steps in my recovery. I mean leaps and bounds. Things are still hard but I am still fighting and I am winning. My dear friend Tina texts me with an invitation; she says her church's youth group is looking for a poet to perform at a youth event. I automatically want to say no. She told me the theme for the night was "running from God." I sighed; there was no mistaking the feeling I had. I had to do this. God wanted me to do this. I prayed about it this time. When I started to doubt myself, doubt God I asked for more faith, for confidence and strength. When I was unsure of what to say I asked for guidance and clarity and peace. God delivered. A few weeks later I stood on that stage, spotlight and all, gave my anxiety to God and I shared a few hopeful poems. I shared a poem about running from God and how I was ready to come home. I felt redemption and pride and so much grace.

The point in sharing this story is to remind you, and myself that if you miss an opportunity, or even slam that door shut, God does not lock it and throw away the key. Your worst moments, your worst days, your shortcomings, your mistakes, your fears don't have to define you. They are not the main event. They are not the headline. They do not describe you as a whole. They are not the chapter your story has to end on. I have so many more pages after that panic attack in Lauren's arms.

God had so many more plans for me. He helped me get to a job that I love. I work with people every day. That is amazing. He helped me get my license. It took me 6 tries. I can now drive out of state. That is amazing. He helped me write two books, helps me read them out loud. My voice shakes less every time. That is amazing. He helped me stand on that stage a comeback story. That is amazing. I am proud of myself. I am proud that I've (mostly) stopped running. I am proud that while I am still struggling, I will not accept defeat. I will not back down from this fight. There is so much more story for me to write. I have so much left to say, so much left to share. My story doesn't end here.

IT IS A
PRIVILEGE
TO BE ON THIS
STAGE
THANK YOU
GOD
FOR CHOOSING
ME.

1P57

People can change.
Time does heal.
Things will get better;
they can always turn around.
I don't want to rush myself.
I don't want to quit before my time is up
because I used to be afraid to leave my house,
talk to strangers,
get behind the wheel;
I could not even walk to my mailbox.
It is a poem in itself
that I leave my town,
drive to Virginia,
stand in front of people I have never met,
and share hope in the form of poetry.
So please, listen closely.
God has more plans for you.
You have more chances for things to go right.
You have more time for them to get better.
You have to keep trying.
Find a way to hold on.
I will help you.
I promise it's worth it
because after every show,
I say goodbye to my new friends in Virginia,
get in my car and drive home,
and the first thing I do is check the mail.

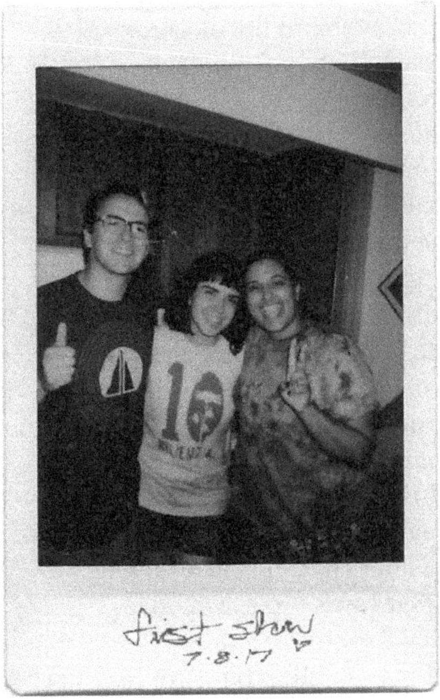
first show
7·8·17

I am, I am, I am

I want to be steadfast in my belief
that God can always hear me,
that He knows my voice well,
that He always wants what's best for me,
that His plans are always to prosper and never to harm,
that His timing is better than my own,
but I have doubts.
I am Thomas.
I am Jonah looking for a place to hide.
I am Peter and there is crowing in the distance.
I am Lot's wife and I can't help looking back.
I want more faith than fear.
That's been so hard lately,
and by *lately,* I mean the past 16 years.
I am still learning. I continue to grow. I am trying to trust
but there is still so much work to be done.
I have to stop forgetting that God never takes time off.
He never takes leave from me.
I need to remember He is listening when I'm on my knees
screaming at the heavens that, "This just isn't fair!"
and when I'm whispering, "I can't do this anymore"
and when I'm thinking He can't hear me,
when I feel alone in this.
He is listening when pain has left me speechless.
I am at a loss for words but He can hear a feeling;
the feeling in my gut that I was too ashamed
to admit out loud.
It sounds like, "God, I am scared to be more like Your son.
I am scared that it will hurt too much.
I am scared that I hurt too much.
I am scared that I'm too fragile for this,
that I'm not strong enough for You.
I am scared You ask too much of me."
I plead, "Please stop asking so much of me."
You answer my cries and my whispers and my fears.
You say, "I am, I am, I am, I am here.
I am listening.
I never grow tired of teaching you
the lessons that you are so tired of learning.
Let me take this weight from you

before you can collapse.
If you're not ready,
I will wait. I will pick you up from the floor.
I will raise you up onto your feet.
I will teach you how to walk again.
I will pull you out of the valley.
The valley is not your home.
I am your home.
You feel sick over this because you miss me,
because you tried to hide from me,
because you tried to do this on your own.
You always try to do it on your own
but I am here.
I am listening.
I am, I am, I am, I am here."
God, when anger's got control over my tongue,
You hear me out.
You do not turn away from me.
When pride holds me back from You,
You wait for me with open arms.
I want to be devoted. I want to be Ruth.
I want to be unrecognizable like Paul
after he changed his name.
I want to trust You enough to be so vulnerable
that I would use my tears to wash Your son's feet.
I want to be Job. I want to be Job so badly.
When everything is taken from me
I want You to be enough.
I want more faith than fear.
I want to be steadfast in my belief
that You have and will always be here.
You prove it every day.
You tell me,
"I love you through the doubts and the fear,
the anger and the pride.
I am, I am, I am, I am still here."

Where The Heart Is

In spite of it all, I rejoice.
It's the light of it all I call home.

joy

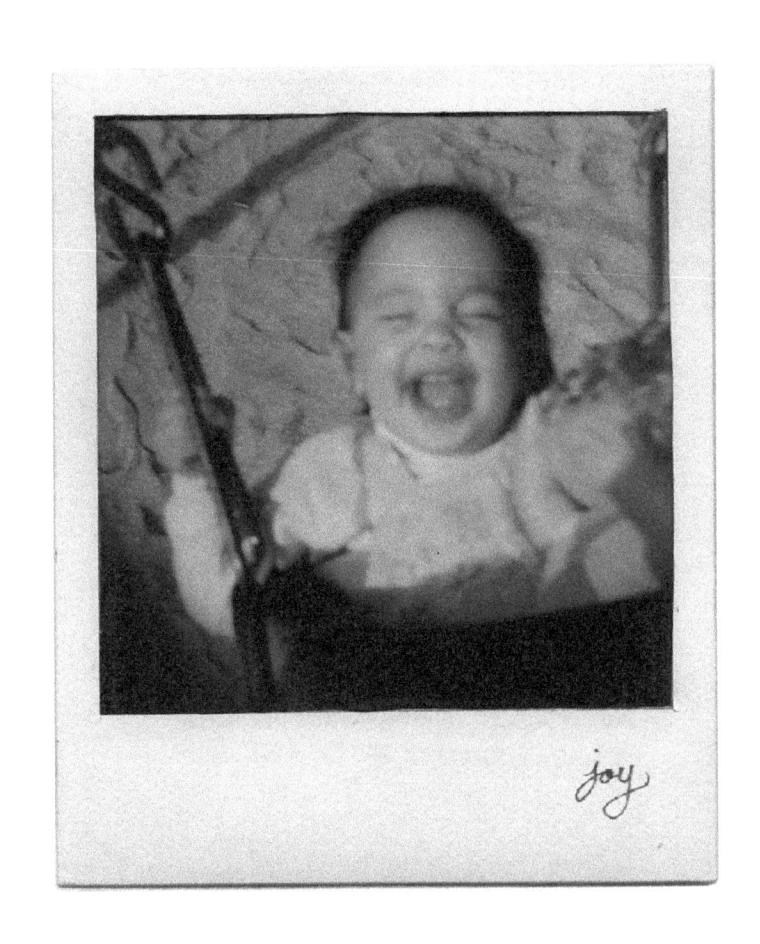

acknowledgments

Mom, every book, every poem, every word that I will ever write is dedicated to you. When you tell me to keep fighting you always step in to be my shield. When pain had me at a loss for words you never doubted I had something important to say.

I owe so much to my best friends. Your support rang so much louder in my ears than any fear. Tina, Bethany, Daniel, Kate, Ciera, Brielle, Sadie, Hannah, Devin, Chelsea, Chris and Karla- I thank God for you so often I memorized the prayer.

The Miller family, Joe, Brad, Carly, James, Kori, Emily, Lauren, Stephen, Crissy, Margie, Marion, Jonny, Molly, Joie, Niki, and Maria thank you for caring about these published books just as much as you did when I was giving out crudely stapled together prints off my mom's printer. You and the rest of my friends believed in these books when they were barley a fully thought out plan. I am grateful for all the encouragement that was poured out to me, the prayers, and the relentless support.

Adisu, Sage, Jenna, Josh, and to all the other children I love, I can't put all your names here and you will probably never see this book but you are a light in my life that never goes out and I can't imagine doing anything without acknowledging you.

To everyone who shared my books through social media and word of mouth, left reviews, gave one to a friend, gave me words of encouragement, was touched by anything these poems had to say, I am forever grateful for you. To everyone who came out to a show to hear these poems out loud, I was terrified but you were kind and gentle and you took care of me and made me feel more powerful than my shame.

To all of you I am so thankful. You welcomed me in and asked me to make myself at home. I am, I am, I am.